Response Journals

By Julie Wollman-Bonilla

SCHOLASTIC
PROFESSIONAL BOOKS

New York • Toronto • London • Auckland • Sydney

For Tony,
who always believes in me

And for Gramps,
who always did

Samples of students' work on pages 24, 43, 44, 49, and 58 first appeared in "Reading Journals: Invitations to Participate in Literature," *The Reading Teacher*, 43, 112–120, 1989. They are reprinted with the permission of the International Reading Association and Julie Wollman-Bonilla.

Cover Design by Vincent Ceci
Cover Art by Mona Mark
Design and Illustration by Drew Hires

ISBN 0-590-49137-7

12 11 10 9 8 7 6 5 4 3 2   2 3 4 5/9

Printed in the U.S.A.

Contents

Acknowledgments
5

Chapter One: *Why Response Journals?*
7

Chapter Two: *Getting Started*
17

Chapter Three: *Replying to Students' Responses*
31

Chapter Four: *Dealing with Problems*
47

Chapter Five: *Assessment*
55

Chapter Six: *Activities Related to Response Journals*
71

Bibliography, Suggestions for Further Reading, and Suggested Booklists
80

ACKNOWLEDGMENTS

Many people have helped make this book possible. I am especially grateful to Angela Jaggar for her enduring support and interest. I am also grateful to my editor at Scholastic, Kate Waters, whose enthusiasm and understanding have made writing this book a pleasure.

I am indebted to Linda Korobelnik and Genis Melendez-Delaney. Linda welcomed me into her classroom and shared her thoughts and experiences openly. Genis is a rare principal—remarkably dedicated and open-minded, despite the overwhelming demands of her job. I deeply appreciate her support of my efforts to gather information on how response journals work in real classrooms.

I owe my gratitude to the students whose work appears in this book (and to their parents). Each one gave me permission to collect and publish his or her work, and I have represented the work exactly as it was done. I have, however, changed all names.

I would also like to thank Janet Parrack, permissions editor at the International Reading Association, for her help.

Finally, my thanks to Sara Miranda for patiently playing while I worked on this.

Why Response Journals?

If you teach, you've probably heard of response journals. Response journals are simply written dialogues, or letters, two learners exchange on a regular basis. These letters consist of each one's responses to a learning experience and to each other's responses. Response journals are often used in conjunction with reading. Many teachers have found that journals infuse new energy and interest into their reading programs. This book focuses on reading response journals, but as you read you will able to envision how you might use journals to enhance any activity.

The purpose of this book is twofold. To those who are new to response journals, I present information that will help you decide whether response journals are worth trying in your classroom, show you how to use response journals, and help you to defend your decision to administrators and parents. For teachers who have already tried response journals, I suggest solutions to common problems and discuss how to make journals more effective and responsive to specific needs.

Why Use Response Journals?

Consider what you do when you read. For me it's natural to respond to what I read by talking about it with others. When I read a particularly interesting, boring, shocking, annoying, or confusing text, I want to discuss it with someone else, both to air my reaction and to find out what they think. Whether I am reading the newspaper or a novel, I stop periodically to say to my husband, "Can you believe this?" Or the next day, I remember to ask a friend what she thinks of a text I find puzzling. I think this tendency to make social interaction a part of reading is common. I suspect you will find my behavior familiar.

The desire to express our pleasure or surprise or anger, to ask questions, and to find out if others share our responses may be natural for adult readers. But do child readers also seek social interaction? Are response journals suitable for children? The following sections should help you answer these questions. A look at the research on learning, on the reading process, and on writing·to learn provides strong support for the use of response journals in elementary classrooms.

Learning

Even when we envision crowded classrooms, we tend to think of learning as a solitary experience that takes place in an individual's head. In fact, the work of the Soviet psychologist Lev Vygotsky demonstrates that learning is a social process. Children are guided to deeper understanding and new knowledge through interaction with others who support and at the same time challenge them. For example, teachers support emergent readers by applauding their efforts to construct a story even if they don't follow the print closely. And teachers challenge students by asking them to take a different perspective when they have a strong negative or positive reaction to characters, events, and information they encounter in texts. Interaction with peers can provide the same type of support and challenge for learners.

Although learning is stimulated by social interaction, it is also deeply personal, rooted in each person's unique complex of background knowledge and experience. Learners build on what they know by relating new information to old. James Britton, an expert on the relationship between language and learning, explains that articulating their ideas facilitates students' learning by helping them to explore and organize what they know, integrate new information, give shape to emergent thoughts, and clarify and reflect upon their ideas.

Finally, learning is dependent on a learner's purpose. What students focus on and remember depends on their reason for learning. If a child has no purpose except to meet a teacher's requirements, then he or she is unlikely to integrate and remember information or skills for any length of time.

The nature of learning has important implications for teachers' roles. First, the activities teachers plan must permit students to develop their own purposes. Second, as James Britton argues, because students build upon the knowledge they bring to the classroom, in order to facilitate learning teachers must first understand children's perspectives and be familiar with their prior knowledge and experiences. Interaction makes possible the kind sharing of ideas and experiences that allows teachers to get to know students and helps students to discover what they know and think and to make sense of new ideas.

In most classrooms it is impossible for teachers to have regular, extended conversations with all students. However, such interaction can take place in writing, and response journals are an ideal format for such personal dialogue. Because they are used for authentic communication, response journals are not simply an exercise for the teacher. Students control the content, they can define their own purposes, and they have an audience that values their ideas enough to read and reply to them. Journals validate students' thoughts, provide them with feedback that supports and challenges them, and encourage the type of personal involvement that is essential to learning. There are no right answers or hidden expectations, so everyone can feel confident.

The Reading Process

Thirty years of research on the reading process, by such notable investigators as Ken Goodman and Frank Smith, has established that meaning is not in a text. Readers actively construct meaning by using their prior knowledge and strategies such as prediction to make sense of print. Texts serve as guides, leading readers to recall certain information and, through linguistic cues, suggesting what might make sense in a particular place. But without the knowledge, purpose, and thought processes a reader brings, a text is simply a collection of marks on paper.

Consider an example: If I were reading about air travel and came across the word *fly,* I would draw upon my knowledge of sentence structure to determine that the word was being used as a verb rather than a noun. My knowledge of word meaning would suggest that the word was being used to describe the operation of an airplane rather than a bird's movement. Similarly, if the text read *The pilot controls the bird,* I would guess that the term *bird* referred to an airplane, and I would look for confirmation of my hypothesis as I read on, using text evidence in conjunction with my background knowledge. If I came across a discussion of the bird's nest, I might have to correct my hypothesis.

My interpretation would also be influenced by the context in which I was reading and my purpose for reading. For example, I might be more interested in what I was reading if I were about to take an airplane trip than I would be if I had no such plans. I might also pay more attention to the details of aeronautic engineering if I were preparing for a test, rather than if I were reading just to pass the time in a crowded waiting room. And these details of engineering might mean something different to me if I were a mechanic reading for the purpose of repairing an engine than if I were a fearful passenger concerned about airplane maintenance.

Response journals are well suited to the active nature of the reading process. They invite students to construct personal meaning by building on what they know, reflecting upon the print, formulating hypotheses, and asking questions. Response journals are also conducive to engagement because they encourage students to define their own purposes for reading and to interpret texts personally.

In addition, response journals help students develop mastery of their reading processes. By encouraging them to reflect on how they read, both as they write their responses and as they read their teachers' replies, journals help to develop awareness and control of useful reading strategies.

Writing to Learn

Writing to explore and share ideas can be a powerful tool for learning. Writing not only forces students to articulate their thoughts but, unlike talking, it also allows them to capture and see their ideas on paper. And as Janet Emig has pointed out, because writing is a slower process than talking and lasts longer than speech, it gives students time to reflect on their reading and to organize their developing interpretations. Response journals free students to use a conversational voice, to progress at their own pace, and to focus on ideas rather than mechanics. As a result of their freedom, students are able to explore their ideas and feelings, to contemplate how the text evoked certain responses, and to formulate hypotheses, predictions, and questions about their reading, without worrying about errors.

How Will Response Journals Fit into My Reading Program?

Response journals may be ideal tools for helping students learn about and from reading, but you're probably wondering if you will have to reorganize your entire reading program just to try this approach. Fortunately, response journals are flexible— they adapt to meet students' needs and your goals. Response journals may be used across the curriculum, with a range of reading materials. Journals are well suited to reading in mathematics, science, and social studies, as well as language arts. Finally, journals fit nicely into a range of organizational structures, from independent reading to small discussion groups to whole-class programs.

Response Journals in an Independent-Reading Program

When students are reading either self-selected or assigned texts independently, response journals may be the primary way for them to communicate their ideas and get help on a regular basis. Even if individual conferences with the teacher are part of an independent-reading program, these can rarely be scheduled frequently enough to meet each student's needs. And, of course, a conference does not permit the extended reflection and self-pacing that are integral to exploratory writing.

When used as part of an independent-reading program, response journals also make it easy for you to monitor how much each student reads and what types of books he or she chooses. This information will help you assess progress and guide students to new books they might like.

In an independent-reading program students may exchange responses with their teacher or with their peers. In order to provide an audience and regular feedback for their work, you may want students to write and reply to peers several times a week and to exchange responses with you only once a week or so. Peers may be able to give students more frequent feedback than you can offer. Peers also introduce one another to new texts and offer new perspectives on shared texts. A peer's obvious enthusiasm for a book is often more persuasive than a teacher's recommendation and may spark a reluctant reader's interest.

Response Journals in a Small-Group or Whole-Class Program

Response journals also work well as a component of a program in which small groups or the whole class read the same text and meet to talk about it. Journals help students prepare for participation in a group or whole-class meeting because they can organize their thoughts and articulate their questions beforehand. This preparation is especially useful for students who are less confident about speaking spontaneously or who don't "think on their feet" as well as they do when given time. It is also helpful to have a place to record questions when they arise rather than trying to remember them for the meeting time. And journals are a safe place to ask questions that students hesitate to ask in a discussion for fear of appearing dumb. Journals give students who participate less in group discussions the opportunity to express their ideas, demonstrate their comprehension, and get their questions answered.

When writing a response after a group or whole-class discussion, students have a chance to reflect on what was said during the meeting and develop a deeper understanding of their reading. In addition, students can exchange response journals. Journal exchanges help them become aware of diverse perspectives on the same text and may generate interesting discussions when the group meets.

Will Response Journals Work in My Classroom?

Research strongly suggests that response journals are worth trying. They can help students develop purpose, interest, and skill in reading and a deeper understanding of what they read. Journal writing is also fairly easy to introduce into your reading program— it fits conveniently into any organizational scheme. But you may still be wondering: "What happens when response journals are introduced into a real classroom?" The stories of teachers who have tried response journals at all age levels are testimony that they work. Many of these stories appear in the articles and books listed under "Suggestions for Further Reading" on page 80.

This book is based on my experience with response journals in real classrooms. As a teacher I have used response journals in my own elementary classrooms, and as a consultant I have helped teachers introduce response journals into their reading programs, from kindergarten through grade six. I have seen journals succeed in private-school classrooms serving very privileged children and in public schools in the most socioeconomically disadvantaged neighborhoods in New York City. I have seen students from numerous sociocultural backgrounds experience just the kind of engagement and growth in reading that research suggests they would. My experience has convinced me that response journals are relatively easy to use and work remarkably well in any setting to help children develop as readers. As you read the next five chapters—and encounter the many examples of students' work—I think you will understand my enthusiasm.

The Examples in This Book

The examples in this book come from fourth, fifth, and sixth graders' response journals but could equally well have been taken from younger students. These students represent a range of reading abilities. When they began keeping journals, some were very competent and regularly read for pleasure, but others were very weak readers who read only when forced to.

The students' responses were directed to their teachers, who replied on a regular basis, but they were also used by many to organize their ideas and questions before group discussions or individual conferences and to reflect on what others said during these meetings. Some students actually referred to their journals during group meetings and chose to exchange responses with peers as well as the teacher. This was their option. Others shared their writings with the teacher alone.

The responses used as examples will be easier to understand if you're familiar with the texts students were writing about. The fourth graders were reading the fantasy *Tucker's Countryside* by George Selden (Farrar, Straus and Giroux, 1969), a sequel to the classic *Cricket in Times Square*. In *Tucker's Countryside* Harry Cat and Tucker Mouse leave their home in the Times Square Subway Station to visit their friend Chester Cricket in Connecticut. Chester wants to save his meadow from impending real estate development and Tucker is determined to help him. In the meantime, clever Harry Cat temporarily becomes the pampered pet of a child who lives across the street from Chester's meadow.

The fifth and sixth graders were reading *Bridge to Terabithia* by Katherine Paterson (Crowell, 1977). This is the realistic story of a lonely fifth grader named Jesse who feels alienated from his four sisters, his parents, and his classmates. The only person who really seems to understand him is a girl named Leslie. Her family moves into Jesse's poor, rural Southern community in order to escape big-city life. Leslie and Jesse quickly become best friends and share some wonderful experiences until Leslie dies in a tragic accident, leaving Jesse to cope with her loss.

I have chosen to use examples in the following chapters because I believe that real student responses are the best demonstration of the potential of response journals. Without the students' voices as support, my arguments for journals are empty. However, while these examples represent the work of diverse children, they come from just a few classes. Other students might write very different types of responses. Therefore, don't consider these examples prescriptive. One of the integral qualities of response journals is that they are personal and individualized. Expect each reader's responses to vary somewhat in form, content, and function.

A Student's Voice

I want to end this chapter with the words of one sixth-grade student who told me what she thought about the introduction of response journals into her classroom. She does a fine job of summarizing what I've said:

I think it's really special because you get to think, you get to write, sometimes you don't like to write but it's better to get your thoughts down on paper. Sometimes I go over my responses just to see what I thought and sometimes I change my mind. When the teacher writes back you learn more and see more about the subject because you see another side of it. I think writing teaches us a lot about books instead of the other way, where you have to answer the questions in the basal book.

—Dawn, age 12

②

Getting Started

In the first chapter I argue that it is relatively easy to incorporate response journals into a reading program. However, because journal writing will probably be brand new to your students, you should carefully consider how you will initiate this activity to make it work. This chapter focuses on three key issues in getting started: choosing materials, introducing journals to students, and initial expectations.

What Materials Will I Need?

The only materials necessary to begin response journals are reading materials and a place for students to write and receive replies.

Reading Materials

Response journals can work with any reading materials, including fiction, nonfiction, poetry, essays, short stories, novels, and textbook selections, in any subject area. The only condition is that the reading material has to be interesting enough to evoke some response.

Many teachers find that replacing textbooks with trade books gets their students interested in reading and renews their own interest in teaching reading. Students also often articulate their preference for good literature. As one sixth grader explained to me, "I like these new literature books. Those three-page stories in the basal book don't make sense and they don't teach you anything."

In my experience, response journals work best when students are reading fiction, nonfiction, and poetry trade books, because these are generally more interesting and challenging than textbooks. However, a variety of literature-based textbooks are appearing on the market, and if you are required to use textbooks, response journals will at least encourage your students to develop personal engagement in their reading.

If you are free to choose your own materials and want to find literature that is likely to capture students' interest, there are a number of sources available to assist in the selection process. Some of the best booklists, which include descriptions of texts and often group them by theme or subject, for ease in curriculum planning, are listed at the back of this book on page 80. Whether you are stocking a classroom library with a variety of titles for an independent-reading program or choosing text sets for small groups or the whole class, you can select books that will enhance the success of reading journals in your classroom by using the following criteria:

1. A text should be of interest to students. If students have nothing to say about a text, they will write simply to meet your requirements rather than respond personally. In order to determine what will engage students, consider their age. For example, books dealing with adolescent issues and experiences and with realistic ethical dilemmas will be especially interesting to fifth and sixth graders, whereas fantasies may strike these older students as babyish.

Also consider your particular students' preoccupations and concerns. If you are studying Colonial history and they seem particularly curious about how historians get their information, choose a book on archaeology in the United States. If students seem more interested in the experience of being a child in Colonial times, try to find a book on the everyday life of Colonial children. Try to select books that reflect the concerns of your students. For example, if issues such as group rivalry and rejection by peers often arise, a nonfiction or realistic-fiction selection dealing with friendship might be especially relevant.

2. A text should be high-quality literature. For example, fiction should include full plot and character development, interesting, evocative language, and, where appropriate, realism and humor. Nonfiction should be accurate, clear but not overly simplified, well organized, and written in vivid language. Students may also enjoy books that do not have these qualities—for example, rapidly produced realistic-fiction series in which characters are neither well developed nor realistic. They should never be discouraged from reading these books on their own, but use your reading program to familiarize them with the best literature you can find.

3. A text should be within your students' reading abilities. No matter how appropriate a book's topic or theme seems, if your students have too much trouble reading it, they will not be able to focus on thinking about it. Choose challenging but manageable texts. Of course, the more engaging a text, the more challenging it can be, since interest makes reading easier.

If you want to expose students to a book you think they'll appreciate but is too difficult for them, read it aloud and then let them respond in writing. Reading aloud is also a good option for students who are not yet independent readers.

You may also find it valuable to choose texts that integrate your social-studies, science, mathematics, and language-arts curricula. Immersion in a topic helps students develop interest and a sense of mastery, facilitating a more complete understanding. For example, during a study of immigration, the language-arts program might include Bette Bao Lord's *In the Year of the Boar and Jackie Robinson* (Harper Trophy Books, 1984), or while exploring homelessness, students might read Donna Guthrie's picture book *A Rose for Abby* (Abingdon Press, 1988). Such titles complement nonfiction literature or textbooks.

The Response Journal

Response journals can consist of almost any form of bound, lined, or unlined paper. Students can write in a composition book, a spiral notebook, or any other book or booklet. If they choose to write on loose-leaf paper it should be bound with a report cover or stapled or fastened together. Journal entries and subsequent replies should be kept together in chronological order so that students can review them. By informally reviewing their entries, students can gain insight into how they read, become aware of reading strategies that work for them, discover that interpretations can change and deepen with thought, and assess their own progress.

Response journals can also be kept on a computer disk as long as students can use the computer daily, during or immediately after reading. Teachers or peers can then access the responses, read them, and reply on disk. Students often write far more on the computer than they would by hand, especially those who have trouble with the mechanics of handwriting. There is no need to print out the response journal as long as students can access their work anytime they wish. If not, the responses and replies should be printed and bound into a booklet to which new printouts can be added regularly.

Response journals work when they are personal and student-controlled. You can begin giving students control by allowing them to choose or construct their own journals so that they have something they like to write in. Students will spend more time on their writing and will write more thoughtful, extensive responses when they are comfortable with their journals.

How Will I Introduce Response Journals to My Students?

Since response journals may be unlike any activity students have done in the classroom, your introductory explanation of them will be important. Make sure you clearly define and communicate the purpose of keeping journals. Students should understand exactly what their responsibilities are and what is expected of them so that they are free to focus on thinking about the text rather than trying to guess what you want.

One of the best ways to communicate what response journals are is to show students a sample first. The response you share may be your own or one written by a student in another class. Choose a response that reflects at least some of the range of possibilities inherent in journal writing, or compose a sample response. Preferably it should be a response to a text students know. Write an honest response that reflects what you thought as you read. Try to include questions you had, feelings the text evoked, and reflections on your reading process, such as, "I wasn't sure what the author meant by *disciplined* until I kept reading and saw that Bonnie always works hard, practices a lot, and pushes herself to do her best in school and in baseball."

Introduce your writing as one type of response, not a definitive model. Suggest a variety of possibilities for the content of students' responses. Then ask them to brainstorm their own suggestions, making sure they know that they are free to move beyond these possibilities in composing their own responses.

Some Suggestions for Responses

1. **What you liked or disliked and why**
2. **What you wish had happened**
3. **What you wish the author had included**
4. **Your opinion of the characters**
5. **Your opinion of the illustrations, tables, and figures**
6. **What the text reminds you of**
7. **What you felt as you read**
8. **What you noticed about how you read**
9. **Questions you have after reading**

Remind students that the journal is a place to record their reactions and questions, not a place to simply summarize what they've read, although a summary may be included in some students' responses.

Encourage students to write while they read or to return to the text while writing. Looking back and copying phrases or sentences from the text will help them better understand what they've read and how it shaped their reactions. If you looked back as you wrote your sample response, tell students about it.

Showing students your own or another person's response journal as a sample also helps convince them that spelling, mechanics, and neatness don't matter, as long as their work is legible. Point out that the sample includes elements such as ideas crossed out and added in, and that its organization reflects the writer's train of thought rather than careful planning.

It is essential that students understand there is no right answer or proper topic to write about and no particular form their responses should take. Keeping the journal is a requirement, and students will be expected to write responses on a regular basis, but responding is not simply an exercise to please the teacher. Response journals are intended to permit authentic communication of students' own ideas to a real audience from whom they will get a reply. Of course, students need to know exactly what you expect of them. For example, will you require that they write a response each day during the reading period, or several times a week? What if they have not finished the assigned reading—should they still write a response? Can they write at home, or must the responses be completed in school? What will happen if they don't keep up with the writing? How will you assess their work? Your requirements and expectations must be determined in advance and made clear to students if they are to be comfortable with the relatively open-ended guidelines for content.

What Can I Expect?

Because response journals are so open-ended, students' initial responses may vary enormously in quality, length, and commitment. Remember, this is probably a brand-new activity for them, and some may view it as an opportunity to avoid doing any work. Others may write responses that reflect uncertainty about expectations, fear of thinking the wrong thing, or a desire to please you. Give students time to learn that you do expect serious attention to response writing and that you really do want to know what *they* are thinking. This may be the first time anyone has ever asked them to do more than guess what the teacher is thinking or what the textbook authors consider the right answer. It may take weeks for students to adjust, so be patient.

Common Types of Responses

If you are trying response journals in your classroom for the first time, it may be reassuring to have some idea of the types of responses you can expect. I have illustrated some typical responses below. The examples are excerpted from longer responses.

Common responses include:

1. Opinions about the plot and characters or about the information presented in a text. For example, Leanne's response:

I think that the men, Sam and Lou were nice because they understood the kids wanting the meddow.

And Alonso's response:

At the starting a guy throws something out of his car Leslie called out to him Litterbug and I agree with Leslie Litterbugs are destroying our environment. people who litter are stupid and dumb and I think there should be a penalty for litterbugs because our environment is in jeopardy because of these people.

2. Expressions of enjoyment, boredom, compassion, or anger.

Two examples follow:

I wish that I could stop the rain. I feel so sorry for Tucker and Chester. I also feel sad because they ran out of food.

I couldn't believe how low down people can get like Ellie and Brenda to call Leslie a stick and not a girl.

3. Comments on the language or literary techniques used, such as Samantha's observation:

I think it is very realistic the way the author discribed how Tucker got all frantic.

4. Comparisons of the text with the reader's life. For example:

In this chapter Jess and Leslie like to talk a lot during class, I know I talk in class but they talk on Leslie's father working with money and going to washington but one thing that Leslie talks a lot about is making a secret magic kingdom for themselves. I have conversations about what we are going to do at lunch time and stuff like that but they talk about totally different things.

5. Predictions, such as:

When Tucker said "facinating in fact" and so on I was sure he had a plan, I think he will tell in the next chapter.

6. Articulation of expectations for a particular type of text. For example, Anthony's comment on what he expects in a fantasy adventure:

This chapter needed more strengh and more action.

7. Reflections on the reading process. For example, Mira tells how she solved a comprehension problem:

There's one part I don't understand is a sentense on page 6 where it says, You shouldn't ought to beat me in the head and went off obediently to fetch his T-shirt. After I read it over and over again I understood it.

8. Questions about vocabulary, language use, plot, information, characters' behavior, and the author. For example:

Then the next morning he eats a large breakfast but why? Mostly when somebody dies like a friend or family member you don't want to eat at all.

Of course, your students' responses may differ from any of the examples I've provided. One reason for these differences is each student's personal style of responding.

Different Styles of Response

Personal preferences and characteristics influence how students respond to texts. Some students display their feelings openly while others are shy and hesitate to share their thoughts. Some write lengthy responses while others always write little. Students' different interests may also affect the way they respond to a particular text.

Perhaps even more powerful than individual personalities are the effects of students' sociocultural backgrounds. Research has established that students' sociocultural backgrounds profoundly influence how they carry out school tasks. For example, Shirley Heath, a researcher and teacher educator, found that black working-class children are taught at home that it is inappropriate to tell a person what he or she already knows. Unlike middle-class children, these students hesitated to display knowledge that seemed apparent or to respond to questions that seemed to have obvious answers. As a result, if they were writing responses to a text, they might have appeared to lack comprehension even when they understood their reading very well.

Other research on students from various sociocultural backgrounds suggests that referring to their lives outside of school, in the context of the classroom, is considered inappropriate by some. Consequently, they may never write responses comparing texts with their own lives. Similarly, students from certain backgrounds learn to view texts as authoritative and unquestionable. They may focus on making sense of the text and backing up their assertions with textual evidence rather than critiquing or exploring their reactions to what they read.

Sociocultural norms are so deeply ingrained in all of us from birth that we are generally unaware of our own assumptions and expectations. This makes it difficult for us to recognize that others may have been raised with different ones. Yet these norms are central to how students use their response journals, so we have to develop awareness and appreciation for differences among students. As a start, consider a few very different responses and what they reveal.

Alonso began each of his responses with a summary of the chapter's events:

In this chapter its Christmas and Jess gives Leslie a puppy and with the illustration of a puppy it's breed looks like a boxer they give him the name Prince Terrein for short, P.T. he's so playful and fun to be with. Leslie wants him to be serious but a puppy is a puppy always jumping, barking, well, always playing.

Alonso's retellings demonstrated his level of comprehension, and he always followed his chapter summaries with a personal comment:

I wish I had a puppy. I had one. His name is Benji he died in the summer, I still miss him but I can't do anything about it, but I'm alright.

Alonso's responses are very personal; his emotional openness is striking:

I like the way they show there feelings in this chapter about the golden room. They would have liked blue but her father wanted gold after they were done painting the room they found out it was a beautiful selection. When the sun shined in the room, the room would sparkle like magic and it was so beautifully expressed that when I read it, it gave me a tingle in my back.

Alonso tended to relate the text directly to his own life, as he did when he wrote of his dead puppy. In contrast, others position themselves as spectators commenting on the text.

Compare Alonso's responses with Jan's:

Why didn't Leslie ever go to church before?? Why would Jess say that church is boring and that Leslie would hate being there?? Why didn't Leslie get mad when Jess squirted warm milk straight out of the cow and into her mouth?? Leslie liked it when Jess did that but when he tried again, and missed, he started giggling and lost his control and squirted her on the ear, but she still didn't get mad, Why?? Why would the people in the church get jealous just because Leslie and Jess walked down the aisle and sit with his family on the first pew and call both of them disgusting??

Both students' responses reflect intense interest and careful thought, but their styles of responding differ. Jan's responses are less personal than Alonso's, she is critical of the text, and she asks many questions.

Even among students who use their responses mainly to ask questions there are differences in style. Consider the format and content of Jasmine's responses as compared with Jan's:

1. *I don't understand what a "dadgum" is page 49, 1rst paragraph.*

2. *I like the way they describe May Bell's tears. She broke up into a "fresh round of sobbing."*

3. *What's a parapet. page 53, 2 paragraph.*

Unlike Jan, Jasmine doesn't retell the story in the course of asking her questions, but this does not necessarily mean she doesn't understand it.

Because students' learning styles and perspectives on how to do school activities vary, their responses will vary. You must be sensitive to these differences and respect diverse perspectives. As you read students' responses, try to understand their intentions and look for evidence of knowledge and learning—even if it's not immediately apparent. At the same time, it is your job to extend students' thinking and introduce them to new perspectives. The next chapter considers how to do this by focusing on your replies to students' responses.

Don't Expect Formal, Edited Writing

Remember that you have asked students to focus on meaning, not mechanics, and to use their journals as a tool for learning rather than as a place to demonstrate their writing skills. Because of the informal, exploratory nature of response journals, students often write quickly. Their ideas and questions seem to flow onto the paper. As a result, it is common to find words and letters left out, misspellings, lack of punctuation, and nonstandard grammar.

In addition, since response journals are like a conversation on paper, students' entries tend to reflect the way they talk informally—nonmainstream dialects and second-language interference may be more evident than in formal assignments. For example, English is Rita's second language, and the word order and tense marking systems of her native Korean are evident in her responses:

I think it was funny how Tucker was complain about Harry. Tucker was say, "I think he's a bum."....I think it was kind funny when Bill Squril asked "What's the next plan." When Tucker hadn't the plan yet.

And Derreck's black English dialect is evident in his responses:

I like that chapter because he start getting in trouble with his friend and that really is where the books start.

It is important to remember that these students are doing exactly what was asked of them—getting their ideas down on paper without worrying about correctness. In fact, it is worth celebrating the fact that students who are well aware that they don't speak standard English are willing to take a chance and share their ideas as freely as Rita and Derreck did. It is unlikely that they would be able to write nearly as much or as thoughtfully if they had to focus their energies on using standard English. Of course, in your replies to students you can model standard English, and conventional spelling and punctuation, as you validate their ideas.

3
Replying To Students' Responses

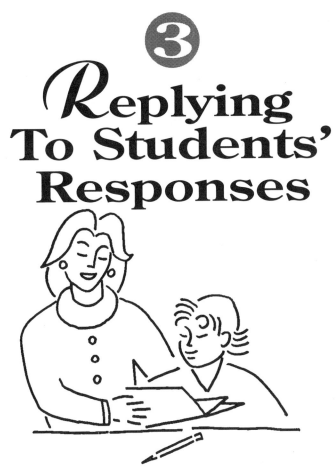

Response journals work because they facilitate dialogue. Your replies to students' responses are as important as the responses themselves. First, by replying you give students the message that journals are not simply a required exercise—they are tools for authentic communication with a real audience.

Second, replying helps encourage enthusiasm for reading and reflecting on texts. Students love to get a reaction to their ideas from someone who cares what they think, and they will enthusiastically share their thoughts and eagerly read your replies.

Finally, replying is crucial, because it is through your replies that you teach. Providing individualized feedback allows you to work with each student at his or her own pace. You can use your replies to meet each one's needs and provide the support necessary to facilitate each one's learning. This chapter focuses on how to reply so that you use this teaching tool most effectively.

How Will I Find Time to Reply?

If you are like most teachers considering response journals, you are probably wondering how much time replying to every one of your students will take. At first it may take you as much as five minutes to reflect on each student's response and consider how to reply, but you will soon find that this process becomes natural and less time-consuming. Even at the start, however, writing replies will take no more time than you would otherwise spend preparing and correcting students' work. When I first introduced response journals in my classroom, I was pleased to discover that replying took me no longer than correcting worksheets or making up questions for students to answer, yet it was far more beneficial for students and more interesting for me.

Of course, if you try to reply to thirty students each day, you will probably be overwhelmed. You need to devise a workable system, which will probably entail replying to only a small group of students each day so that every student receives a reply about twice a week. You may choose to have students write responses only as often as you can reply. For example, they may read independently five days a week and be required to write a response only two days a week. On the other days they may meet for discussion of their reading in an individual conference, with a small group or with the whole class. Or you may decide to have peers reply to one another on alternate days, as long as students agree that peers may read their responses.

One efficient and effective way to organize a reading program including response journals is to divide students into four groups who spend the reading period as follows:

Monday

    Group 1— Read independently and then write a response

    Group 2— Read independently and then write a response

    Group 3— Read independently and then meet for discussion

    Group 4— Meet for discussion and then read independently

Tuesday

    Group 1— Read independently and then meet for discussion

    Group 2— Meet for discussion and then read independently

    Group 3— Read independently and then write a response

    Group 4— Read independently and then write a response

Wednesday

    Group 1— Read independently and then write a response

    Group 2— Read independently and then write a response

    Group 3— Meet for discussion and then read independently

    Group 4— Read independently and then meet for discussion

Thursday

    Group 1— Meet for discussion and then read independently

    Group 2— Read independently and then meet for discussion

    Group 3— Read independently and then write a response

    Group 4— Read independently and then write a response

Each student then participates in discussion twice a week and writes a response and gets a reply twice a week. The fifth day can be used for self-selected independent reading by students while you give additional help to those who need it (more on extra help in Chapter 4). This type of schedule makes replying manageable and provides each student with a variety of experiences, including independent learning, learning through interaction with peers, and learning through interaction with the teacher.

What Should My Replies Say?

The nature of your replies will be important to encouraging students to share their thoughts, feelings, and questions openly without fear of embarrassing themselves. Most important, your replies must show that you can be trusted to read without criticizing and that you are truly interested in what students think.

Students will be unable to learn from your replies if you immediately put them on the defensive by challenging their views. You have to validate their ideas, even though you may disagree with them, before you introduce a different perspective. Consider what Abby wrote about Jess's father's angry reaction when the train set he gave Jess didn't work as he expected:

In this chapter it seems that Jess's parents are spoiling all the fun out of Christmas for him. Like his father not being satisfied on the way the track was set.

Now, consider the following two replies to Abby's response:

Reply 1

Do you really believe that Jess's father ruined Xmas for him? Is it possible he was upset that he couldn't afford better gifts for his children? If he had more money to spend he would have gotten a better train set. I just have to feel that the father is doing the best that he can with a limited income, and he can't hide his true feelings.

Reply 2

It does seem like Jess's father really ruined Xmas for him. I felt like the father was as upset as Jess. I think maybe his Xmas was spoiled too because he couldn't afford better gifts for his children and that's why he got angry. I think he wished he had more money to spend so he could have gotten a better train set. What do you think?

The first sentence of reply 1 challenges Abby's response while the first sentence of reply 2 affirms her feelings before going on to introduce a more sympathetic perspective on Jess's father.

By validating Abby's feelings, reply 2 helps to develop her capacity for response by encouraging her to express and explore her ideas. Because her response is affirmed, the reply also makes it easier for her to open up to an alternative perspective on Jess's father than if she had been put on the defensive, as in reply 1.

Establishing your appreciation for students' ideas helps them get comfortable with exploring their own responses. Equally important, however, is that your replies should help students develop their reading abilities and deepen their understanding of particular texts. You can achieve these goals by using your replies to

1. Share your own ideas and responses

2. Provide information

3. Develop students' awareness of reading strategies

4. Develop students' awareness of literary techniques

5. Model elaboration

6. Challenge students to think in new ways.

Examples of each of these types of response may help you get started in writing your own replies to students.

The following examples are excerpts from real replies to real responses by students. These are not necessarily the best or only replies that would have helped students. As you read you may think of other ways to reply that you prefer. You might even think about how you would reply to each response before reading the reply I've used as an example.

Sharing Your Own Responses

Sharing your ideas and feelings with students, just as they share with you, creates an authentic dialogue and introduces them to a different viewpoint and new information. For example, Ned wrote:

I think chapter six was very exciteing. I am glad Tucker and Chestre did not drown. I thought it was funny when Tucker said to Mrs. Pheasant "I'm glad your husband got such a plump helpmeet."

His teacher replied:

I was really excited and nervous when I read chapter six. I'm glad Tucker and Chester made it, too. Their plan to weigh the branch down was a great idea. I loved when Tucker almost said a "fat wife" and then said "plump helpmeet." That was funny!

Building on the topic of Ned's response, his teacher shared her reaction to the story.

Similarly, when Mira wrote that she found it funny to read that the young music teacher at Jesse's school "was the first teacher in Lark Creek Elementary School to wear pants," her teacher replied:

I remember the first time I wore slacks as a teacher after years of having to wear skirts and/or dresses. It was very strange at first, but I certainly prefer it, especially on cold, winter days.

This reply helped make an unfamiliar situation real for Mira as she learned that not too long ago, in her own school, female teachers were forbidden to wear pants. It also established that her teacher was willing to share her personal experiences and feelings just as she hoped students would.

In the beginning it may be difficult for you to share your responses with students. As adults who may have experienced years of criticism and little opportunity to write authentically in school, many teachers are very wary about expressing themselves in writing. If you don't write easily, or lack confidence in what you write, first remember that your replies will be seen only by individual students. In all of my experiences with response journals, even the most rebellious students have never criticized their teacher's replies. Instead they seem to appreciate and respect their teacher's honesty and openness, even when there is disagreement.

Second, get support from a trusted adult who is willing to read your first replies and provide reassurance and suggestions before you hand journals back to students. Ideally, try to team with another teacher who is using response journals. Ask for feedback on what he or she likes about your replies, and for suggestions on how they might be improved. If you exchange roles and comment on your colleague's replies, this process is less threatening. If you don't have a colleague you can ask for feedback, ask a friend or family member to react to what you've written. Over a short period of time you will grow confident enough to reply without such support, although you may find it professionally rewarding to continue the exchange. Many of the sample replies in this book were composed by a teacher who initially doubted her own ability to reply at all!

Finally, use the examples in this book, and the replies of colleagues who are more experienced with response journals, as models from which to take off. And above all, remember that there is no right or wrong in sharing your reactions. Regardless of what you write, your honest, open replies have intrinsic value because they are authentic and they communicate your respect for students and your willingness to trust them and reciprocate their openness.

Providing Information

Students often ask questions or reveal confusion in their responses. Your replies can provide the information they need to make sense of what they read. Questions about word meaning are very common. When the answer is easily found in the dictionary, you will probably want to refer students there so that they learn how to solve vocabulary problems independently. However, in some cases you may know that a student will have great difficulty figuring out a word's meaning from the dictionary entry. For example, fourth grader Rita asked, "What does wrung mean?" Sending her to the dictionary would have been fruitless because *wrung* is listed under *wring,* a word that Rita doesn't know is related. Instead, her teacher replied:

Wrung is related to the word wring. You can wring out a wet towel by twisting and squeezing it so all of the water comes out. EXAMPLE: When I wiped the lunchroom tables yesterday I wrung out the water from the wet sponge first so it didn't drip on the floor when I carried it to the table.

Wring can also mean twisting and squeezing your hands together like people do when they are nervous or worried. EXAMPLE: "I wrung my hands before the big test." I'll show you with my hands when the group meets tomorrow. Before then, go back and look at the story. See if twisted or squeezed makes sense where it says wrung.

Students also express confusion and ask questions about text meaning in their responses. For example, Jan asked:

On page 34-35 does it mean Leslie didn't have a television set or was she just trying to get out of work?

Her teacher replied:

I don't think Leslie was trying to get out of work by saying she had no television. Remember, her family was trying to begin a new life away from the big city where material things and success were the only things that people cared about. Perhaps the lack of a television set is one way of getting back to true family living—where reading, talking, etc. replaces the electronic age.

This reply answers Jan's question and, simultaneously, models for her the process of inferring an answer from information in the text. Learning to make such inferences will help her answer her own questions in the future.

Developing Awareness of Reading Strategies

Your replies can help students become better readers by making them conscious of reading strategies that they already use and teaching them new strategies. For example, Shellie responded:

When Jess said that he hated Leslie I thought he really didn't mean it. Then I read the end and saw I was right, He just said that because he was mad Leslie was gone for ever and he missed her.

Recognizing that Shellie was using an effective reading strategy her teacher replied:

I see that you had an idea about Jess's real feelings when Leslie first died and then you read on to see if you were right. That's a good way to read anything—make your own predictions or assumptions as you go along and keep looking for evidence that you're right or wrong.

By articulating what Shellie had done her teacher hoped to bring the strategy to awareness so that Shellie could rely on it in the future.

Sometimes students don't mention reading strategies, but their responses lead naturally into a reply that teaches a strategy. As you read students' responses look for opportunities to build on them by suggesting strategies. For example, Ned wrote:

I'm glad I know what kind of person Simon turtle is finaly. I'm also glad I know what the problem is.

Recognizing an opportunity to teach a strategy, his teacher replied:

Yes, the author finally lets us in on the problem. Did you have any idea of what the problem was before we were told? Could you predict what it might be from what you had already read?

This reply introduced Ned to prediction, an important reading strategy. Because the strategy was introduced in a meaningful context in response to Ned's interest, it is likely that he will remember and use it.

Developing Awareness of Literary Techniques

Awareness of literary techniques helps students understand how texts arouse certain responses and what makes them effective. In addition to making students more aware readers, familiarity with these techniques makes reading easier for them, because they know what to expect in a text. Students who are familiar with techniques are also able to try them out in their own writing.

As with reading strategies, look for natural opportunities to introduce literary techniques. For example, Abby questioned the relevance of a particular chapter in one of her responses:

This chapter, The Evil Spirit, to me seems to be an unnecsary and worthless chapter. It doesn't really give any important information related to the story.

Her teacher replied:

Other students have agreed with your opinion about the chapter. The author must have had a reason for including this chapter. Is she trying to prepare the reader for the events that are to happen? What do you think is her purpose?

Without using the technical term, this reply suggests to Abby that the chapter may have been included specifically to foreshadow what follows.

Opportunities to mention literary techniques are not always as obvious as in the case of Abby's response. For example, Ron wrote:

I also liked when tucker figuers out how to save the medow and he jumps up three feet.

Seeing a chance to teach Ron about suspense by commenting further on Tucker's plan, his teacher replied:

I liked this chapter too. It is very exciting when Tucker comes up with a plan. The author leaves you in suspense at the end by not telling what the plan is. He really made me anxious to keep reading.

Similarly, Leanne's teacher saw a chance to build on Leanne's assertion that "this book was great because it really made you care for animals" by introducing the technique of perspective. She wrote:

I'm glad you liked the book. It made me look at animals differently too! They seem so real and nice and sensitive. The author makes us care for them by telling the story from their perspective. We see things and feel things as they see and feel them.

This reply encourages Leanne to think about *why* the text is effective in making her identify with the animals. It also helps her recognize that her response is the result of a careful choice of technique on the author's part.

Modeling Elaboration

In order to use writing as a tool to fully explore their responses and develop their ideas, students need to elaborate on their initial thoughts. You can provide a model for them by elaborating on their comments in your replies.

Fourth grader Ned wrote the following response:

I liked chapter 5 the best of all. I would love to be in Harry cats pozision.

Consider how his teacher's reply built on what Ned wrote:

I liked chapter five a lot too. The author describes the food so clearly you can almost see, smell and taste it. It sounds delicious! And Harry is getting so much attention he must LOVE it! Harry is in a good position.

The reply gives Ned a model of how to elaborate on his

response by exploring what it is that makes Chapter 5 so enjoyable and Harry's position so enviable.

In addition to modeling elaboration, your replies can also encourage it. For example, when Anthony wrote, "I like when Tucker through a fit and when the man walked by," his teacher replied:

I liked Tucker's fit, too; it was funny! I never expected a mouse to want to PACK before leaving.

The part where the man walked by really stood out for me. I really liked that part because it gave a human's-eye-view of the situation. What did you like about it?

By concluding with this question, the teacher encourages Anthony to think further about why he enjoyed the part "when the man walked by" and perhaps to elaborate on his initial response in his next journal entry.

Challenging Students

You can open students' minds and enhance their understanding by challenging them to take new perspectives on issues they raise in their responses. Of course, your challenges should never invalidate a student's personal response. However, by guiding them to reconsider their initial reactions, you may help students come to a deeper understanding of texts and of their own responses, and an awareness of the complexity of issues.

One way to help students broaden and deepen their understanding is to ask them to consider the implications of their comments. For example, when Jasmine wrote, "I know that Jesse's father is trying to be supportive, but I think he's not doing the best he could do," her teacher replied:

What more do you think he could do for Jess? Would any words have changed what Jess is feeling? What do you think he should have said or done?

By asking Jasmine to articulate specific possibilities, her teacher challenged her to explore the implications of her response.

Similarly, Oscar's teacher challenged him to consider the implications of his belief that "Jesse will become the fastest kid in the fifth grade because determanation, dedecation and desire pay off." She replied:

Do hard work, dedication and desire always result in finishing first? Is finishing first an important goal to strive for? Why?

This reply encourages Oscar to explore his own assumptions as well as think about Jesse's reasons for practicing so hard.

Asking students to imagine characters' thoughts and feelings is another way of challenging them to gain a new perspective. For example, Gail commented on the part of *Tucker's Countryside* where young Ellen, who lives across the street from the meadow that is being made into a housing development, convinces a steam-shovel operator to stop tearing up the land. Gail wrote, "For Ellen to ask him to stop took guts." Her teacher replied, "What gives Ellen the courage to ask him?"

This question encourages Gail to think more about Ellen's motivation and about why people do courageous things in general.

Your replies can also help students broaden and deepen their understanding by taking the perspective of a character other than one with whom they automatically identify. For example, Anthony wrote, "I felt sad when I read that Ellen lost harry," and went on to comment on how glad he was that Ellen had a new friend—a pet chipmunk. His teacher replied:

A chipmunk seems like a neat pet. Even though Ellen lost Harry she has a new friend.

How do you think Harry feels about having to leave Ellen?

This question asks Anthony to consider Harry's feelings as well as Ellen's.

You can also challenge students by asking them to form personal opinions on text events and information, and on characters' behavior. For example, Alonso wrote:

In this chapter Jess goes to Washington and he keeps repeating that he should have brought Leslie. Why?

His teacher replied:

Should Jess feel guilty about going to Washington, D.C., without Leslie? What do you think?

This reply asks Anthony to form his own opinion about Jesse's behavior. Replies that challenge students to explore their beliefs, take a new perspective, or articulate their opinions help them develop new insights into what they're reading and into their own reactions.

A Final Note on Replies

Despite my simple categorization of replies for the sake of clarity, few replies fit neatly into a single category. For example, look again at Ned's teacher's reply:

I liked chapter five a lot too. The author describes the food so clearly you can almost see, smell and taste it. It sounds delicious! And Harry is getting so much attention he must LOVE it! Harry is in a good position.

Although Ned's teacher intended primarily to model elaboration, this reply does more. It simultaneously introduces a literary technique and shares her own response. Most of your replies will be multifunctional, even though, like Ned's teacher, you may be consciously focusing on one function.

I've suggested some ways of replying to facilitate students' learning, but the categories above are not exhaustive. There are many ways to reply that are in keeping with the basic goals of validating and extending students' thinking and helping them grow as readers. As you consider your particular students' responses and determine their needs, you can reply to them in ways that you feel will best help them learn and help you achieve your curricular goals.

What Are My Replies Really Saying?

Your written feedback can help students learn about reading, about literature, about writing to learn, and about themselves and their world. They can help *you* learn about your feelings and your attitudes. Your replies also contain subtle messages that are as powerful as the more obvious content. Some of these messages are contained in the form. For example, if your writing is difficult for students to read, they may feel that you don't care enough about communication to take the time to write legibly. On the other hand, if you are sure to write in a way that your students can read easily, you will show them that the response-journal dialogue matters to you and that you expect them to attend to your replies as closely as you do to their responses.

Look critically at the hidden messages in your responses, as well. One teacher who asked for my help in improving her response-journal program was concerned because her students seemed to be using their responses simply to summarize the plot of the stories they were reading. She wondered why this had become a pattern after she had stressed to students that the journals were a place to share their responses and opinions, not simply to retell the story.

A look at her students' journals showed that she was inadvertently encouraging a focus on plot through her replies. For example, after a student wrote, "I liked the end of the chapter because Nora overcame her fear and was ready for the challenge," the teacher replied, "What happened next? Did she accept the challenge?" Another student wrote, "I couldn't believe Nora decided to compete in the contest," and the teacher replied, "Did she compete? How did she do?" This type of reply gave students the message that their teacher wanted them to summarize what happened.

It is extremely difficult to critically evaluate your own replies, but you can look back at what you've written over a period of several months and search for patterns. Do you always ask students what they think will happen next? Do you often reply with a subtle denial of students' ideas, such as, "Well, maybe you're right, but..."? Do most of your replies include evaluative comments, for example, "Good...," suggesting to students that there are better or worse or right and wrong responses? If you find a pattern, consider what the underlying message is.

Another way to determine what your responses are really saying is to look for patterns in students' responses over time. If all of your students tend to write the same types of responses, gushing praise, for example, the reason may be your replies. Students may be writing to please you based upon what you have written back to them in the past. Examining your replies and students' responses will help you recognize how students are interpreting what you write and will suggest how you might modify your replies.

4

$\mathcal{D}$ealing with Problems

Many students find response journals a welcome relief from less meaningful, less interesting exercises such as answering comprehension questions or filling out workbook pages. But others may resist writing responses or may be confused by the freedom that journals seem to offer. Problems can also arise when students simply have trouble writing or when their responses reflect considerable difficulty understanding their reading. This chapter focuses on how to deal with these various problems.

How Can I Overcome Resistance and Confusion?

Students who dislike reading and writing, or who view journals as a break from "real work," may resist reading and responding. In order to overcome this problem, first make clear to students that although they are free to choose the form and content of their responses, reading and responding are requirements. Second, make reading and responding more appealing (and educationally effective) by helping students feel confident about their work, by choosing appropriate texts, by guiding students to develop personal involvement, and by being flexible enough to make changes in your program when response journals don't seem to be working.

Make All Students Feel Competent

Often those who dislike reading are slower readers who feel incompetent because of their inability to keep up. You can overcome their resistance by ensuring that success with response journals is unrelated to students' reading abilities. Don't penalize slower readers by requiring that they finish their reading assignment before writing a response. This is unnecessary. Students can read at their own pace, use the final five or ten minutes of the reading period to write a response to what they've read, and complete their reading assignment at another time during the school day, or at home if they choose.

Similarly, let those who struggle to write, and proceed slowly, take their time. Make sure students know that the length of their responses is irrelevant. You are interested in quality. One of the benefits of journal writing is that it is individualized and self-paced so that all students can feel comfortable and competent.

Choose Appropriate Texts

The best way to engage students who are simply reluctant readers is to choose books that are manageable for them and will capture their attention. As I urged in Chapter 2, search for texts that relate to students' interests. If you can't purchase new books, try to find appropriate ones in your classroom, school, and community libraries. Often you can create a text set for a small group by pooling copies of a book owned by your school library with those from your public library. Many public libraries allow extended loan periods for teachers. Sometimes other teachers have copies to lend as well.

When students complain, as fourth grader Ron did, "I really have nothing to wright about," it may be because the content or level of difficulty of the text they are reading is inappropriate for them. Don't be afraid to decide together with students that a text isn't worth sticking with. Reading should function to inform or entertain; there is no point in reading just for the sake of reading when there are plenty of wonderful books, short stories, essays, and poems available that will give students pleasure and increase their knowledge. If you have access to a selection of texts, you can increase students' investment in reading and writing about their reading, by letting them, individually or as a group, choose what they will read.

Remember, however, a text is not necessarily inappropriate if students don't love it, as long as it arouses some reaction. Criticism is as valid a response as praise. For example, Anthony wrote:

I thught this chapter was dull because there was not alot of action and it was sort of personal in a way...The turtle talked too much and talked about boring things like his friend and what happened to them.

From this response it is clear that Anthony understands and cares about what he's reading. Of course, a steady diet of books that students consider dull will not develop their enthusiasm for reading, but occasional criticism is to be expected.

Guide Students to Develop Personal Involvement

"I have nothing to write" or "This chapter was okay" are obviously not complete responses. A less apparent but more common problem is students who write lengthy entries but don't respond to their reading. Consider Oscar's journal entry:

In this chapter May Belle's father bought her twinkies and she showed it of and then later Janice Avery stole them, so they decide to get even or pay her back.

What they did is write a fake love note to get Janice Avey upset so they could get even.

She liked Willard Huehs so they spread a rumor that she likes Billy Morris.

When they got her mad they felt that they had gotten even with Janice Avery.

This summary reflects excellent literal comprehension but little thinking beyond that. It is not really a response. Whether the reason for this was resistance or confusion about the purpose of journals, Oscar's teacher wanted to help him move beyond summarizing.

She used her replies to encourage Oscar to respond personally:

I'm reading the book along with you so it's not necessary to summarize the chapters.

What do you think about the way Jess and Leslie tried to get back at Janice? Do you think they got even with her?

This reply lets Oscar know that journals are intended for authentic communication of an individual's ideas; they aren't an exercise to prove to the teacher that you understand. Like Oscar's teacher, you can help students develop engagement in their reading by guiding them to respond personally. It may take time and many replies before students like Oscar move away from simple summaries to personal commentary. Be patient but persistent.

Depending on the age level, some students (particularly upper graders) may include *very* personal and private information in their responses. Being aware of this possibility will help you decide on an appropriate course of action for your group of students.

Be Open to Making Changes

Problems don't always stem from the text or students' attitudes. Sometimes students resist responding because they are bored with the reading-writing cycle itself or because the journal process is not meeting their needs. For example, they may feel frustrated by the fact that they never really have a chance to reply to your replies, because when they get your replies they've already read a new section of the text and they have to respond to that.

If response journals have been successful in your classroom but they no longer seem to be creating excitement about reading, it may be time to make some changes. Remember there is no single, right way to use journals. You have to do what works for you and your students. There is no honor in sticking with a system that's not working.

You may need to assign more or less reading or have students write more or less often. You may try having students exchange responses and reply to one another if they haven't been doing so. You may decide to give students time to reply to your replies before they are expected to write a new response. You may decide to alternate roles with students—sometimes they respond and you reply; at other times you respond and they reply. Whatever you do, try not to get so comfortable with any routine for response journals that you begin to see it as the only possible way. Instead, continue to experiment to find out what works for you and your students.

What Can I Do If My Students Have Trouble Writing?

Problems with response journals may also arise when students have difficulty writing to communicate because of their stage of literacy development or motor development. Students who do not yet write conventionally can record their responses using invented letters, invented spellings, and drawings, but you may have a difficult time understanding their messages and replying. Nevertheless, you can still establish a dialogue. Students can read their responses to you individually and you can reply with a few sentences written on the spot, as you say them aloud. Or you and other helpers such as aides, student teachers, volunteer parents, or older children can act as the students' secretaries. After students have written their responses, they read them to a secretary, who writes their messages in conventional form underneath the original. You can then read the responses and reply later. If you use secretaries, be certain not to devalue students' invented writing. Instead introduce the conventional form as "another way of writing it," "the way I write it," or "the way it would look if it were in a book."

Both of these approaches to accommodating children who are still learning to write conventionally will allow students to respond personally to their reading, to explore the use of writing to communicate, and to see conventional written forms modeled.

Another potential problem is older students who know how to write conventionally but are hindered by their weak motor skills. For such students, simply forming letters is a difficult chore, and they make their handwritten work as brief as possible. When given a typewriter or computer, however, they are freed of their problem and can write lengthy responses without the stress they experience writing by hand. If your students don't have access to computers (and you don't have a classroom typewriter), try asking parents or businesses in your community to donate an old but usable one. Response journals can work for students of all ages and abilities as long as *you* work to accommodate students' needs.

What Can I Do If My Students Have Serious Comprehension Problems?

In Chapter 3 I argue that your replies are a powerful teaching tool that can clear up students' confusion and help them better understand what they read. Sometimes, however, a student's response reflects comprehension problems that appear to be serious. For example, Helena wrote:

Leslie has no Television. that's how I get the hint that Jesse's town is poor.

It seemed Helena had completely overlooked the information that Leslie is new to Jesse's community and far from representative. Her parents are quite wealthy and have given up their television set on principle.

Understanding that Leslie is a relatively sophisticated outsider in Jesse's town is important to understanding the friendship between Jesse and Leslie and the effect Leslie has on Jesse's life. The gap in Helena's understanding needed to be filled because this information is central to the book's plot and theme. However, this need could not be met in a reply alone.

Similarly, when Sonia wrote, "I just finished ch 9 and I didn't understand it alot," her response signaled that she needed more help than a reply could provide. Both Helena and Sonia needed a teacher to sit down with them and discuss the story at length, looking back at particular sections as they talked.

By giving students extra attention when they need it you can get some insight into the root of their problems and help them overcome specific difficulties. For example, if you went over Chapter 9 with Sonia, you could get a sense of whether it was the extensive dialogue in the chapter, the shifts in perspective, the imagery, or her hesitance to use background knowledge to construct meaning that was causing Sonia's problem.

In order to make response journals work for every student, set aside a small amount of time each week, perhaps a free reading or catch-up period, when you can give extra attention to students who need it. Of course, extra attention shouldn't always be the result of problems. You may want to meet with a student one-on-one just to talk further about an interesting issue he or she raised in a response or to express your pleasure at the growth you've observed in his or her journal. Extra attention shouldn't be viewed as a penalty for problems but as a way to provide help, reassurance, and praise beyond what you give in your replies.

⑤

_A_ssessment

As with any classroom activity, it is important that you assess what students are learning by keeping response journals. Assessing students' work will help you to recognize what they know and do effectively as readers, to monitor their progress, and to plan instruction that is responsive to their needs. Assessment will also provide you with concrete information to document the growth of particular students and the effectiveness of response journals in general. This information will be important evidence for yourself, and for administrators and parents, that response journals are working. Information gleaned from close attention to students' response journals, and excerpts from their journals, can be an important component of a portfolio of children's work that you use for assessing progress.

Why Use Response Journals for Assessment?

It makes sense that students' daily reading and writing should form the basis for any assessment of their abilities. Yetta Goodman uses the label "kidwatching" to describe informal observation of authentic, functional literacy activities. She argues that you can learn a lot more from observing what your students actually do from day to day in the classroom than from formal tests given once or twice a year. This position makes sense intuitively, and teachers who rely on kidwatching instead of testing find that it really does provide them with more accurate information.

Because there is no right or wrong response, and all opinions are accepted, journals are a nonthreatening context in which to share ideas. This means that students will show you their best— they won't be afraid to take risks, venture ideas, ask questions, and construct personal meaning. On the other hand, when faced with unfamiliar tests, they are more likely to fear being wrong and to "play it safe" by trying to figure out what you're looking for.

What Will Response Journals Tell Me?

Responses will reveal whether students understand what they are reading and will give you insight into their reading processes, their knowledge of literature, and how engaged they are in their reading. Students' responses will also grant you insight into their personalities and lives—even at times serious issues in their lives that might require special attention. Because response journals can help you assess students in each of these areas, you can uncover and address specific problems and build on strengths to help students grow as readers.

Comprehension

Basic comprehension or comprehension problems are usually readily apparent in students' responses. For example, Helena demonstrated her understanding of the characters' situations when she shared her opinion:

I think Janice was much more unfortuned as she played off.

Easter Leslie was dressed up but she wasn't as unfortuned as she played off. I think Janice needed somebody to talk to.

So did her father.

Helena recognized that although Janice appears to be the more fortunate character, she has a terrible problem—her father abuses her. In contrast, though Leslie usually dresses like a needy child, her home life is comfortable, both financially and emotionally.

Comprehension is dependent upon students' reading processes, their knowledge of literary elements and techniques, and their attitudes about reading. A student's responses can illuminate the reason for comprehension problems and the type of instructional guidance he or she needs.

Reading Processes

Readers construct meaning by using linguistic cues and reading strategies. Making sense of print involves linguistic cues from three interrelated language systems—graphophonic, syntactic, and semantic. Graphophonic cues, or letter and sound patterns, help a reader who knows the word *laugh* to figure out the word *cough* by hypothesizing that the final *gh* makes an "f" sound. Syntactic cues consist of phrase or sentence patterns, such as word order. For example, from the sentence "The rodent ate the food," a reader who knows that nouns usually precede verbs may guess that a rodent is some type of animal or person. Semantic cues are meaning cues. In a sentence about an orchestra, a reader might encounter the unknown word *oboe* in the phrase "The person who plays the oboe..." and predict that it is an instrument because that makes sense. Efficient readers use all three types of cues, selecting and integrating information from each linguistic domain.

You can often tell which linguistic cues a student relies on to solve reading problems by considering his or her responses. For example, Gail revealed that she uses meaning cues to help her make sense of texts:

In the beggining where they talked about musican I forgot what it meant but then when John Robin said "Im a pretty good singer my self" it helped me to understand what it meant.

Gail looked to the semantic context, reading ahead in search of relevant information. If reliance on meaning cues alone were a pattern in her responses, her teacher might help Gail by pointing out that there is also a graphophonic cue here—the base word *music*—which is useful in figuring out the meaning of *musician.*

Jasmine's response journal reveals that she is comfortable using all three types of linguistic cues. In the following entry, she was commenting on a passage in which the word *little* is written "le-etle" to reflect the way it is spoken:

I think the word le-etle on page 22 in the first paragraph is another old fashion word [these New York City students considered rural, Southern accents and language to be old-fashioned] that means leathle. Like lelthe weapon. But I know it's not.

Jasmine seems to have found that the conclusion she drew by using graphophonic cues was not consistent with the syntactic or semantic cues in the phrase "just a le-etle." *Lethal* doesn't fit grammatically, nor does it make sense. While she couldn't solve her problem independently, her entry shows that she integrates all three cuing systems when she reads.

As the examples of Gail's and Jasmine's work suggest, recognizing linguistic cues is only one step in constructing meaning. Both girls had to apply reading strategies to make use of linguistic information. Readers build understanding by forming hypotheses, or predictions, and confirming or correcting these as they progress through texts. Response journals provide a window into how students engage in this process. Although they are usually written after reading, many responses reveal the strategies students use while reading. For example, Brad demonstrated that he forms hypotheses as he reads:

I like the way the author said that red mud was slooching up the bottom of his sneakers. because there was holes on the bottom. that made me think Jess was poor.

Brad hypothesized that Jess is poor because of the holes in his sneakers.

Often students share the process whereby their hypotheses were confirmed or corrected. For example, Mira revealed that she formed a hypothesis about Jess that she later corrected as she read:

I also thought that Jess was a girl which I was wrong because he's a boy.

In order to form and confirm or correct predictions or hypotheses, readers must draw on text evidence and their prior knowledge. Students' responses can help you figure out whether they are relying upon information from both of these sources. For example, Mira revealed that she looked to the text for evidence upon which to build and confirm a hypothesis about Jess's emotional state:

I couldn't believe that they had Leslie creamated and most of all how Jess smacked May Belle then when he ran to the creek and through the paints and paper away then I knew he was terribly mad and sad.

The information that Jess threw away his precious paints and paper helped Mira understand how badly he was feeling and make sense of why he hit his favorite sister, May Belle.

Similarly, Abby used text evidence to help her make sense of the relationship between Jess and his father:

This chapter had many things that answered some of my questions. The question that I was still confused with, was if Jess and his father get along and if they liked each other. But when on page 12 it says that he wasn't pleased and that he said, "What are they teaching in that damn school," I was disappointed. Jess had very high hope that his father would be proud of him, but instead it turned out totally different.

In the first sentence of this excerpt, Abby actually articulated that she looks to the text for information that will help her make sense of the story.

Readers must also draw upon the knowledge they bring to texts to construct meaning. For example, Rita used her prior knowledge of how women react to mice in order to make sense of Mrs. Hadley's behavior:

Mostly all women are afraid of mice so thats why Mrs. Hadley screamed.

Similarly, Brad drew upon his prior knowledge to form a hypothesis about the former owner of Leslie's puppy:

On page 67 I think Prince Terrien had a mean master because Jess would sometimes sneak down to the Perkins place and see Prince Terrien crying.

Brad used his knowledge of pet dogs to make sense of why a puppy who is not well cared for and loved would cry.

By studying students' responses you can often discover their reading strategies. You may even find that some students are able to articulate the strategies they use to construct meaning. For example, Brad wrote, "That [the description of Jess's sneakers] made me think Jess is poor," suggesting that he consciously formed a hypothesis by integrating text information and prior knowledge. While not necessary, such awareness of strategies is helpful because it may make it easier to deliberately select and apply these strategies when confusion arises.

Knowledge of Literature

Knowledge of literature is a special type of prior knowledge that helps readers form expectations for texts and appreciate how they work. It is a tool that can help students make sense of any literary text. Response journals can tell you which literary elements and techniques your students notice as they read and which ones you need to introduce to them.

For example, Jan clearly appreciates how a story's language can help create a setting:

Jess, Maybelle, and Miss Bessie all sound like country names. I think that Bridge to Terabithia is about friends that are from the South.

Oscar expressed his appreciation for the power of literary language to create a picture and mood:

I really like the part about the Ten Commandments when the water swept up the Egyptians. I really like the way it was written. Quote "it was an awesome sight...the long dry bend of the creek was a roaring eight foot sea" and the funny part "the hungry waters licking, leaping the banks, daring them to try to confine it."

Oscar noticed and admired the author's use of figurative language.

Jan commented on the same technique, although she mislabeled it:

The terms "Ellie's voice was sweeter than a melted Mars Bar" and "Sweating like a knock-kneed mule" are funny idioms. This book is filled with idioms.

Another of Jan's responses shows that she is aware that authors use description to create realism:

The author used real-life commercial items as she mentioned U-haul, Wide World of Sports, Mars Bars, and others. It makes the book seem realistic.

She also commented on how the author used description to create memorable characters:

The teacher, Mrs. Myers, is described like a witch. The author says that she has a double chin, lemon smile, and is not an understanding person.

Students responses might also mention special techniques used in plot development, such as foreshadowing. Though she didn't know the formal label, Helena's journal shows that she recognized this device:

In Easter it gave a clue that Leslie was going to die. May Belle said, "What would happen if Leslie die?"

When students mention such literary devices you can then build on their knowledge by introducing the formal terms to describe the elements and techniques they notice.

Engagement in Reading

Perhaps the most important information you can glean from students' response journals is whether they are interested and involved in their reading. Without engagement, mastery of the reading process and knowledge of literature are empty skills and information, and students are unlikely to read beyond school assignments.

One sign of engagement is questioning. When students ask questions, they are showing that they care about what things mean. Jan's question in the following excerpt demonstrates that she was involved in the story and was trying to make sense of what puzzles her:

Leslie is a rich kid and she doesn't have a T.V. is it because the T.V. would bother Judy and Bill? Or is she not allowed to have any T.V.'s in the house?

Responses in which students relate texts to their own lives also signal interest and involvement. For example, Brad compared himself with the main character in *Bridge to Terabithia*:

I also realized that Jess is like me because he likes to run and I like to run and he is in the 5th grade and so am I.

Just as Brad suggested he could relate to Jess personally, so did Mira:

In this chapter I thought it was cute because Jess was in love with his music teacher...I remember one day when I had a crush on a teacher.

Other responses reflect engagement by demonstrating that students care about a book's characters. For example, Mira feared that Jess was going to be beaten up by the school bully:

I almost went nuts if Jess was going to fight Janice because if he did everybody knows what will happen.

Students also reveal involvement in their reading when they share opinions and evaluations of a text. As Candice wrote:

I'm done with the book Bridge to Terabithia. So far its one of the best books I read. I thought Katherine Paterson should of wrote more telling about Janice Avery and her father, if he still beat her or if he stopped. And I think Katherin Paterson should of told more about what Leslie father did. If moved back to Washington or if he stayed there and visited Terabithia.

While they may not always be positive, evaluations show that students care enough about a book to have developed their own opinions on it.

How Many Responses Do I Need to Look At?

Throughout this book I have focused on individual responses in order to illustrate a variety of points, but a single response will be of little help to you in assessing students' learning. Instead, you will want to focus on the patterns that emerge over time. For example, Brad customarily wrote lengthy, detailed responses that reflected his involvement, understanding, and knowledge of literature, but consider his entire response to Chapter 11 of *Bridge to Terabithia:*

I didn't like this chapter because Leslie died.

His teacher recognized that he probably responded in this way because Leslie's death was too disturbing for him to be able to write more about this topic.

It's inevitable that students will have days when they're tired or distracted and that they will find certain chapters less interesting or more difficult to respond to than others. It would be a mistake to treat any individual response as if it reflected the range and depth of students' abilities, knowledge, or engagement. The only way to accurately assess their work is to look at each response journal as a whole.

What About Errors?

As you read students' journals for the purpose of assessment, don't forget that you've invited them to share their ideas and ask questions without concern for correctness. Use your responses to model standard English grammar and conventional spelling and punctuation, but don't let students' deviation from your standards interfere with your assessment of their progress in reading.

Of course, responses must be legible and understandable, but as the examples throughout this book demonstrate, students can communicate their meanings regardless of whether they follow your conventions for writing. Although it might be difficult, try to overlook what you would consider errors in a final draft and focus on meaning.

At the same time, in order to fairly assess students' responses, try to accept and respect various different ways of responding. As I argued in Chapter 2, students' personal qualities and sociocultural backgrounds influence how and what they write in their journals. On the surface, some responses may appear to reflect far more knowledge, understanding, and engagement than others because they are closer to your expectations for how a response will look.

Consider one of Candice's responses:

Why did Jesse name dog prince terein and make him a guardian of Terabithia, and he is too little, and why she called the dog dumb and be proud.

This response isn't easy to read because it isn't as explicit and organized as we might expect. Moreover, on the surface it seems simply to consist of questions (without any question marks!) signaling a lack of understanding. However, consider what Candice is demonstrating here, beginning with her strengths. First, it's clear that she understands what happened in the chapter—Leslie declared her new puppy, Prince Terrien, guardian of Terabithia. She did call the dog dumb, though she said it affectionately. In fact, she was very proud of her pet, as Candice mentioned. Candice's response also shows that she had done some thinking about the story. For example, she wondered if a small puppy would actually make a good guardian. Of course Candice's response also suggests that she needs help understanding Leslie's feelings and interpreting her comments.

By looking for students' strengths first you will resist the tendency to misjudge their work, as it would have been easy to do in Candice's case. Study students' responses closely, always looking for signs of what they know or can do as a reader. Of course, you will want to identify each one's needs as well, but starting with the strengths can help you keep your focus on meaning instead of letting surface-level errors distract you.

Can Students Participate in Assessment?

You can also get some insight into students' progress by asking them to assess their own work. After looking over their response journals, students can write their own evaluations, choosing their own foci. This will help you understand what they think is important and may make you aware of progress you hadn't recognized.

STUDENT SELF-EVALUATION

1. When I come to a word I don't know I _____
_____

2. When I come to a sentence I don't understand I _____
_____

3. While I read I usually think about _____
For example, _____

4. I expect a good book to have _____

5. A good author makes sure to _____

6. I feel that reading is _____

7. My feelings about reading have changed because _____
_____

8. What I do best as a reader is _____

9. What I would like to do better as a reader is _____
_____

10. I feel that writing in my response journal is _____
_____

11. I feel that reading my teacher's replies is _____

You can also have students assess their work by filling out a form, like the one below, which elicits information on the categories you're interested in.

Remember, it's far more difficult to articulate what you do as a reader than to do it, so be ready to explain and discuss each probe with your class.

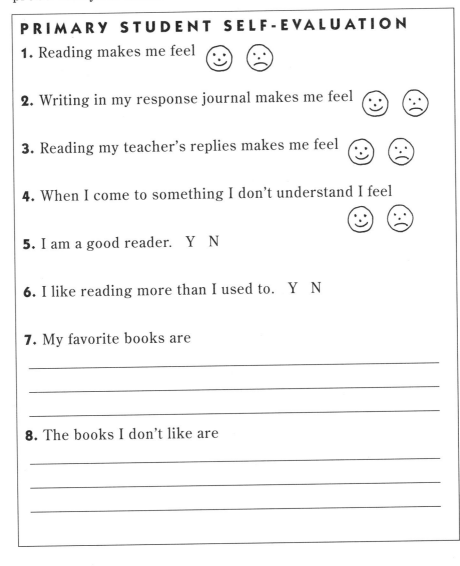

PRIMARY STUDENT SELF-EVALUATION

1. Reading makes me feel

2. Writing in my response journal makes me feel

3. Reading my teacher's replies makes me feel

4. When I come to something I don't understand I feel

5. I am a good reader.   Y   N

6. I like reading more than I used to.   Y   N

7. My favorite books are

_____

_____

_____

8. The books I don't like are

_____

_____

_____

Of course, these probes need to be modified depending on students' age. Very young students will need a form that requires less reading and writing.

Questions that require longer, more specific answers (such as "What do you do when you come to a word you don't know?") will have to be asked and answered orally.

Students frequently have remarkable insight into their own strengths and weaknesses that will complement your observations. Giving students a voice in the evaluation process will also increase their investment in the journals and their sense of responsibility for their own learning.

How Will I Keep Track of All This Information?

Assessment must be systematic and well documented if you hope to accurately evaluate your students and use the results to plan instruction and defend your use of journals. The best system for keeping track of students' progress is one you design specifically to provide the information you seek and to fit your record-keeping style. For example, if you know your students have developed effective reading strategies but are concerned about their engagement in reading, you are unlikely to find a checklist on reading strategies very useful. However, you may want to keep track of signs of involvement in their responses.

Daily anecdotal notes are one form of record keeping that can be very helpful in identifying progress. For example, here is an excerpt from Rita's page in her teacher's notebook:

Rita

11/22 demonstrated comprehension of the animals' problem, expressed real concern for characters in her journal, wrote "I hope it stops raining"

11/25 commented on how she would feel if she were Tucker, understands that he is under pressure to come up with a plan to save the meadow

11/26 many vocabulary questions, needs help with strategies for solving some of these problems independently, really loved final chapter, very enthusiastic response, very happy about outcome for animals

Over time, patterns that are helpful in identifying students' progress emerge from such notes. One clear pattern in Rita's responses was her engagement.

You can jot down anecdotal notes at the same time as you sit down to write your replies to students. However, if you find it too time-consuming to record notes regularly, you might design checklists, listing each type of behavior or knowledge you are interested in assessing across the top of the page and students' names in a column going down the page. Then you can place a check mark or record a date in the appropriate box each time you observe evidence of a specific strategy, knowledge, or attitude. Leave room for brief notes as well. On the next page is a sample checklist for assessing students' reading processes.

Other checklists might focus on students' attitudes about reading (e.g., eager to read, enjoys discussing texts, recommends books to peers, enjoys writing in journal...), or their knowledge of literary elements and techniques (for example, aware of characterization techniques, appreciates descriptive language, mentions setting, notices foreshadowing, comments on plot development...).

Anecdotal notes and checklists need not be used only on an ongoing, daily basis. An alternative approach to assessment is to gather students' responses over time (for example, a month or two) and consider them as a body of work. While this will leave you with a lot of writing to consider at once, it is feasible if you focus on only a few students each week. You can then record your observations in anecdotal or checklist form. This approach may help you get the big picture more easily, but it may also result in a delay in addressing each student's needs.

No one approach to assessment is ideal. In order to balance the pros and cons of various approaches to assessment you may want to combine them. For example, use a checklist on a daily basis and record anecdotal notes as you look over students' work on a bimonthly basis. Experiment with a variety of approaches until you find one that works best for you. Remember, just as it will take time for students to adjust to keeping response journals, it will also take some time for you to work out the best way to document your observations of their progress.

READING PROCESSES CHECKLIST

	USES GRAPHOPHONIC CUES	USES SYNTACTIC CUES	USES SEMANTIC CUES	PREDICTS	CONFIRMS	CORRECTS	
GAIL	10/2 11/1 11/9		11/17 11/23	9/19 11/21	9/19 11/21		9/19 uses background KNOWLEDGE TO PREDICT
JEAN	9/26	9/26	11/1	9/26 10/4 10/7	9/26 11/3		11/3 uses text evidence to predict and confirm
TED	9/13 9/28	11/3	10/1 10/4 11/16	9/13 9/19	9/19	10/7	9/19 very aware of his own strategies — articulates them!
RITA	11/3		9/13 9/19 9/30	9/16 10/4 11/3	10/15	9/16 11/3	10/1 second language seems to create problems using syntactic cues

6
_A_ctivities Related to Response Journals

Response journals help students develop interest and proficiency in reading, and they can also lead directly to other activities that will enhance students' literacy growth and your growth as a teacher. This chapter describes just some of the activities that naturally grow out of response journals.

How Can I Make Connections Between Response Journals and Discussions?

In the first chapter I suggested that students can use their response journals to prepare for discussions of reading material, and that some students may actually refer to their journals during discussions. You can take advantage of the potential for journals to enrich discussions by watching for opportunities to make connections. As you read each student's responses, look for questions, topics, or comments that strike you as particularly important or interesting to bring to others' attention and explore in greater depth. You can then bring these up during the next individual conference or group meeting.

Referring directly to a student's work is fine in an individual conference. You can say, "I see you wrote that you were confused by Jesse's behavior in this chapter," without embarrassing a student, because the conversation is private. However, when speaking to a group, you will have to avoid identifying individuals, or they may begin to fear being open about their ideas and questions in their responses. Make your references to journals general. For example: "I noticed that many of you felt angry about what happened in this chapter, and I found that interesting." Let the discussion take off from there. By deliberately making the connection between written responses and discussions you facilitate the sharing of ideas among peers and initiate discussion of particularly important issues that have been raised by students.

What Other Activities Grow out of Response Journals?

Students' responses sometimes suggest natural extension activities. As you read their journals, look for opportunities for extensions that you feel might interest them and help them grow as readers. Several possibilities are described below.

Letter to the Author

After reading the chapter of *Bridge to Terabithia* in which Leslie's death is explained, Sonia wrote:

I don't understand how Lesily died cause they said she fell of the rope and hit her head on something and that isn't really explain nothing.

And in her next entry she wrote:

And I still think they should explain more about her death.

Similarly, one's of Abby's responses included her opinion:

I just don't understand why the author would suddenly write that Leslie is dead.

These responses are a perfect opportunity to suggest that Sonia and Abby write to the author to ask why she chose to make Leslie's death so abrupt and sketchy.

There are many benefits to writing a letter to the author:

1. Students recognize that authors are real people like themselves.

2. Students' enthusiasm for reading often grows when they get a letter back from an author.

3. Students' own writing may improve as they recognize that writers make deliberate choices and consider their audiences.

4. Students may find it easier to think of interesting topics for their own writing if the author shares with them how he or she comes up with topics.

In addition, writing a letter gives students practice with a different type of writing than informal response. They will have to edit for grammar, spelling, and punctuation, and be explicit enough about their ideas that they can be clearly understood by a stranger.

Note: Be sure students understand that although some authors may respond, many do not have the time to do this. You might want to find out beforehand whether the author in question does respond to student-written letters.

Research Project

Another extension activity is a small research project.

Leanne responded:

Like Ellen, I always wondered if animals speak. I mean I sort of feel that they have a secret language.

Because of her interest, she might want to look into the issue of animal languages by doing a little reading on this topic, perhaps choosing just one or two animals to focus on and then reporting back to her peers. The benefits of such a project include

1. Experience searching for books on a specific topic

2. Experience searching for information within each book by using the table of contents, index, headings, and skimming

3. Experience reading expository texts to complement fiction

4. Experience integrating information from various sources to answer a question.

Mathematical Survey

A third extension activity that is often suggested by students' responses is surveying and recording others' reactions or opinions. For example, Jan wrote:

If Janice took the younger graders milk money, then why wouldn't one of the girls tell the principal or teacher??

Exploring this question lends itself to a survey of people's opinions on what a younger student should do when harassed by an older student. In doing such a survey a student would

1. Have to design a survey question or questions and create options to offer respondents

2. Practice interacting with others to gather information

3. Be exposed to a variety of perspectives on the issue that might help her to understand what happens in the text

4. Use math skills to interpret and represent the resulting data in a graph or chart.

This activity could also involve looking at how survey data are reported in magazines and newspapers, providing experience with a special type of expository reading.

Author or Illustrator Study

Students' responses frequently reflect particular interest in a book's author or illustrator. For example, Ned wrote:

I thought the picture on page 121 is very funny. I really like the pictures in this book.

This response suggests that he might be interested in doing a study of the book's illustrator. This study could involve searching for other books with the same illustrator, comparing the illustrations, and researching how he decides which scenes to illustrate and what media to use.

Similarly, a student might express curiosity about an author and his or her other books, and this might lead to an author study, comparing several books by the same author and gathering information on his or her life and writing process.

An author or illustrator study helps students grow as readers by

1. Introducing them to a wider range of texts

2. Building their knowledge of literary elements and techniques

3. Encouraging them to develop their own criteria for what makes a book good

4. Involving them in reading reference works on the author or illustrator to complement their other reading.

As response journals become established in your classroom other extensions will suggest themselves naturally.

Planning for Extension Activities

Activities that grow out of response journals may be entirely optional and spontaneous, undertaken as the opportunity arises, or you may require that students do an extension activity every month or two, based on one of their responses. Of course, students are likely to learn the most from an activity that they choose to do. If you require an extension activity, let students choose their own project. The more choices they have the better, so ask students as a group to brainstorm a variety of possible extensions, and always be on the lookout for new possibilities as you read students' responses.

How Do Response Journals Relate to Students' Other Writing?

Throughout this book I have suggested that one of the benefits of using response journals is that students will develop a better understanding of the qualities of literature and this knowledge will influence their own writing. You can help students make the connection between what they read and what they write by encouraging them to borrow elements and techniques they notice. For example, Samantha wrote:

I think it is very interesting the way Chester got introduced in the book.

Her teacher replied:

It is interesting the way Chester was introduced by his animal friends before he actually showed up. Do you think this technique might work in the mystery story you're writing? I know you're trying to make it more mysterious. Would it help to have your main character be introduced through the eyes of others before she ever shows up?

Students' responses can also influence their writing by giving them ideas for topics, plots, and characters. For example, many of the fourth graders who read *Tucker's Countryside* were so intrigued with the book's characters that they tried writing stories with talking animals.

Although the examples I've used come from students who were reading fiction, the same types of connections are possible when students are reading expository material and writing reports or essays. Your replies can encourage students to borrow techniques that they notice, such as methods for organizing material, the inclusion of graphics, and the use of rich, descriptive language to enliven difficult subjects.

Can Response Journals Contribute to My Professional Growth?

Most teachers who begin using response journals find that they enjoy teaching more and think they know their students better because of the journals. You can enhance your professional growth by capitalizing on the fact that journals are a rich area for classroom research. As the chapter on assessment suggests, there is a great deal you can learn about individual students, and about the use of journals in general, by examining your own journal program.

Doing research is different from gathering information for the purpose of assessment, however. In assessing students' work, the questions you are trying to answer and the scope of your attention are largely predetermined. As a teacher-researcher, you have the freedom to narrow your data-gathering to match your particular interests, and to let your focus evolve as questions naturally arise in the process of looking closely at journals. You can take the time you need for extended reflection, free from concern about forming quick conclusions and meeting assessment deadlines. Teacher-research will give you a different perspective on what's happening in your classroom, it will develop your powers of observation, making assessment easier and more accurate, and it will allow you to participate in a professional exchange if you choose to share your findings with other teachers.

Because there is so much to be learned from even one student's work, it is probably best to start small. Choose one or two students who interest or puzzle you and focus on their work initially. Give yourself plenty of time to pore over their responses, looking for significant patterns and forming questions. For example, you might find after reflecting on Dan's work that he always responds very emotionally. In contrast, Melissa seems more dispassionate in her responses. You might wonder, What are the reasons for this difference? Do highly emotional responses necessarily reflect greater engagement? Do students who respond emotionally appear to learn more from their reading, or is their progress somehow hindered by their stance? Do I reply differently to students depending upon the nature of their responses? Do my replies seem to reinforce students' stances?

In order to answer these questions you would need to continue studying Dan's and Melissa's responses and your replies, looking for information that bears directly on your questions. It would help to make copies of all of their responses and your replies so that you can make notes on them and even color-code sections with a marker (for example, use green highlighter to indicate phrases that reflect engagement and use yellow highlighter to mark evidence of reading progress). This coding will help you organize your observations into categories related to your questions.

You could complement information in students' journals by considering Dan's and Melissa's contributions during discussions. You might even want to interview both students to find out their views on the purpose of response journals and what they feel they are learning. Of course, new research questions or more interesting paths may emerge during this process and you may decide to alter your focus.

The outcome of this type of research is that you will know more about your teaching and about how you might better meet students' needs. For example, if you found that emotional involvement seemed to promote growth in reading, you could encourage such involvement for all students.

As a teacher-researcher, immerse yourself in students' work, keep an open, questioning mind, and give yourself plenty of time to reflect. You will find that doing research makes your own work more exciting and enhances your teaching and your students' learning.

BIBLIOGRAPHY

Britton, James. (1982). *Prospect and Retrospect: Selected Essays of James Britton* (G. M. Pradl, Ed.). Montclair, NJ: Boynton Cook.

Emig, Janet. (1977). "Writing as a Mode of Learning." *College Composition and Communication, 28,* 122–128.

Goodman, Ken. (1984). "The Reading Process: Theory and Practice." In R. E. Hodges & E. H. Rudorf (Eds.), *Language and Learning to Read: What Teachers Should Know About Language* (pp. 143–154). New York: University Press of America.

Goodman, Yetta. (1985). "Kidwatching: Observing Children in the Classroom." In A. Jaggar & M. T. Smith-Burke (Eds.), *Observing the Language Learner* (pp.9–18). Newark, DE: International Reading Association.

Heath, Shirley Brice. (1983). *Ways with Words.* Cambridge University Press.

Smith, Frank. (1982). *Understanding Reading: A Psycholinguistic Analysis of Learning to Read* (3rd ed.). New York: Holt, Rinehart & Winston.

Vygotski, Lev S. (1978). *Mind in Society: The Development of Higher Psychological Processes.* (M. Cole, John Steiner, S. Scribner, E. Souberman, Eds.) Cambridge: Harvard University Press.

SUGGESTIONS FOR FURTHER READING

Atwell, Nancy. (1987). *In the Middle: Writing, Reading and Learning with Adolescents.* Upper Montclair, NJ: Boynton/Cook.

Atwell, Nancy. (1987). "Writing and Reading Literature from the Inside Out." *Language Arts, 61,* 240–252.

Fulwiler, Toby. (1987). *The Journal Book.* Portsmouth, NH: Heinemann.

Graves, Donald H. (1989). "Research Currents: When Children Respond to Fiction." *Language Arts, 66,* 776–783.

Mayher, John, and Lester, Nancy. (1983). "Putting Learning First in Writing to Learn." *Language Arts, 60,* 717–722.

Staton, Jana, Shuy, Roger W., Peyton, Joy K., and Reed, Leslie (1988). *Dialogue Journal Communication: Classroom, Linguistic, Social and Cognitive Views.* Norwood, NJ: Ablex.

SUGGESTED BOOKLISTS

Lima, Carolyn W. (1985). *A to Zoo: Subject Access to Children's Picture Books.* New York: Bowker.

Monson, Dianne L. (1985). *Adventuring with Books: A Booklist for Pre-K to Grade 6.* Urbana, IL: National Council of Teachers of English.

Sutherland, Zena and Arbuthnot, May H. (1986). *Children and Books.* Chicago: Scott Foresman.